Introduction

The most important player on any football team is the quarterback. He is the man who calls the plays in the huddle. After the teams line up, he takes the ball from the center. Then he hands the ball off to a running back. Or he throws a pass. Once in a while he runs with the ball himself. A lot depends on him.

A top quarterback has to be smart so he can call good plays. He has to be strong because he gets tackled very hard. He needs a powerful arm so he can throw long passes.

This is the story of one of the greatest quarterbacks of all time: Joe Namath of the New York Jets.

Sports Hero

Joe Namath

by Marshall and Sue Burchard

G. P. Putnam's Sons • New York

For Wendy and Marshall, Jr.

We wish to thank Rose Szolnoki, Larry Bruno, and Marcia C. Gauger for their interest.

PHOTO CREDITS

Larry Bruno, pp. 18, 24
Miami (Florida) Department of Publicity and Tourism, pp. 48, 50
New York Jets, pp. 2, 61, 72, 85, 87
Rose Szolnoki, pp. 6, 10, 11, 14
United Press International, pp. 41, 52, 66, 70–71, 82, 90, 92, 94
United States Steel Corporation, p. 9
University of Alabama, pp. 29, 31, 33, 38, 45
Wide World Photos, pp. 44, 55, 56, 58, 63, 74, 76

Contents

Young Joe Namath (center) with his sister, Rita, his father, John, his mother, Rose, and his brother, Bob.

1

The Boy from
Beaver Falls

Joe Namath was born in Beaver Falls, Pennsylvania, on May 31, 1943. Beaver Falls is a town near the city of Pittsburgh. Joe was the youngest of five children. He had three brothers and one sister.

Most of the men who lived in Beaver Falls worked in the steel mill. Joe's father worked there too. For forty years he made steel pipes for boilers.

Joe's father did not like his job. The huge furnaces that melted the steel gave off a lot of heat. And the noise from the machines was deafening. But making steel was the only thing Joe's father knew how to do. So he kept working hard in the mill to earn money for his family.

One day Joe went with his father to visit the steel mill. He saw the flames belching out of the furnaces. He felt the heat. He heard the noise. He was scared. He decided he never wanted to work in a steel mill like his father.

Joe's family lived in one of the

Mr. Namath worked in a steel mill like this one.

Joe's grandmother.

poorest parts of town. The street
they lived on was only a dirt road
with lots of rocks in it.

The wages Joe's father earned at
the steel mill were very low. He

made just enough money to feed his
five children, but there wasn't much
left over for toys. So Joe and his
friends thought up many ways to
earn extra money.

They searched for interesting junk
and sold it to a nearby junkyard.

His mother.

Sometimes they found empty soda pop bottles. They took the empty bottles back to the grocery store and collected a penny for each one. Or they shined shoes for ten cents a pair.

Once in a while Joe worked as a caddy carrying golf bags. The bags were very heavy. Many of them weighed even more than Joe did. He earned six dollars a day being a caddy. That was a lot of money.

Joe had time for play too. He went swimming in a river, which was nearby. He and a friend built little racing cars and drove them in neighborhood races. The cars had no motors. But they could go very fast coasting downhill.

The children in the neighborhood played war on hills made of dirt and trash. Joe and his friends would climb to the top of one of the hills. Then they would try to keep other boys from getting to the top. Sometimes the other boys would charge up the hill throwing rocks. Joe and his friends would duck and throw rocks back.

Joe loved sports most of all. When he was only five, he started playing football in the neighborhood playground. His father helped teach him how to play. Soon Joe could throw the football a long way.

Joe also played baseball with his big brothers. His brothers threw the

13

ball very hard. Joe's hands hurt from catching it. Sometimes his hands hurt so much he ran home in tears. "Stop crying," his father told him.

Joe and his big brothers: Frank (left) and Bob.

"Go back and show them that you can catch anything they throw." Joe did. He also showed them that he could throw the ball pretty hard himself. By the time he was seven, Joe was pitching for the Beaver Falls Little League team.

2
Big Days in High School

When Joe went to junior high school, he tried out for quarterback on the football team. He made the team but not the starting lineup. He seemed too skinny to be a really good football player.

Then came the first game. In the middle of it, the starting quarterback broke his wrist. The coach sent Joe in to take his place. Everybody saw how good Joe was. From then on, he was the first-string quarterback.

When the football season was over, Joe played basketball. And when the basketball season ended, he played baseball. He was good at everything.

When Joe went to high school, the same thing happened all over again. He tried out as quarterback for the varsity football team. He made the team, but he was the smallest player on it. So he spent almost the whole season on the bench. He did much better in basketball and baseball that year.

Beaver Falls hired a new football coach when Joe was a junior. The

coach's name was Larry Bruno.
Coach Bruno could see that Joe
might become a great football player,

Coach Larry Bruno was a friend.

skinny or not. He let Joe play more often.

The coach became Joe's good friend. Joe was not making very good grades in school. The coach wanted him to work harder in class. So Bruno bet Joe a milk shake that Joe couldn't get a B in math. Joe wanted to win the bet, so he began studying more. The next term he got a B in math and won his milk shake.

By his senior year Joe already was a well-known athlete. In fact, he had become famous all over the state of Pennsylvania. The thing he could do best was pass. He was also a good runner. And he was great at faking. He would pretend to hand the ball off to one of his teammates. Then he would zigzag all over the field so no one could catch him.

In one game, the Beaver Falls Tigers played the team from New Castle. New Castle was so good that Beaver Falls hadn't made a touchdown against them for twenty-six years. Joe told his coach, "Don't worry. I'm going to have one of my big days." He did. He passed for one touchdown and scored two more himself to help the Tigers beat New Castle by a score of 39–0. Everybody in Beaver Falls was proud of the way Joe led the team to victory.

Beaver Falls won game after game that year. Soon Joe and his team-mates got very excited about their winning streak. They decided to do something to celebrate.

They climbed up a tall pole on top of a building in town. At the top of the pole was a big balloon with a sign printed on it. The boys painted TAKE 'EM TIGERS on top of the sign. Then they climbed down as fast as they could.

Some people saw them and called the police. The police were going to arrest the boys, but the owner of the building laughed and said to let the boys go. If Joe and his friends had been arrested, that would have been the end of the 1960 Beaver Falls football team.

The strongest team Beaver Falls had to play that year was Ambridge High School. From the beginning of the game the whole Ambridge team went after Joe. They smashed into him as hard as they could.

Finally a bad thing happened. Joe was tackled. He hit the ground heavily and hurt his shoulder. The coach wanted to take him out. But Joe said he was okay.

His shoulder hurt too much to pass, so he faked and ran instead. The Tigers beat Ambridge by a

At Beaver Falls High School the football schedule is posted right outside the front door.

score of 25–13. Beaver Falls was still undefeated.

Joe went to see a doctor after the game. The doctor took X rays of Joe's shoulder. He told Joe that he

The team that won every game during Joe's senior year in high school.

could not play again that season. Joe was heartbroken.

He went to another doctor. The

new doctor said Joe should rest a few days but could play again in a week. This made Joe very happy. Even though his shoulder hurt him for several more weeks, Joe played anyway. Like all good players, he wanted to compete even when he was hurt.

Beaver Falls played nine games in Joe's senior year. They won all nine games. They were the best team in the state. They were rated Number Six of all the high school teams in the country.

As for Joe, he had completed 7 out of every 10 passes he had thrown. He had passed for more than 150 yards a game. He had thrown 11 passes for touchdowns. That was an amazing record. It was no wonder that many colleges wanted him to come and play for their teams.

3
Going to Alabama

It was hard for Joe to know which college to pick. Fifty-two of them invited him to visit. His mother complained that Joe was never at home. He was always flying off to see another college. He finally decided to go to the University of Alabama.

Joe chose Alabama for several

reasons. He liked warm weather. He wanted to play on a good team. But most of all, he wanted to work with a great coach. The Alabama football coach, Paul "Bear" Bryant, was known as one of the best coaches in the country. His football teams were always among the strongest in the nation.

Joe arrived at Alabama looking very snappy. When he met Coach Bryant, Joe was wearing a loud-checked jacket with broad shoulders, sunglasses and a straw hat with a pearl pin stuck in it. He had a toothpick dangling from his mouth.

People in Alabama did not know

what to think of him. They were not used to people who wore flashy clothes like Joe. They also thought

Joe lived with other athletes in this dormitory at the University of Alabama.

he bragged too much about how good he was. People figured that maybe Joe would not be a good football player. They thought he might be just a big joker from the North.

Joe did not have a very happy time his first year at Alabama. Not only did he look different, but also he thought differently. Joe told his Southern classmates that he had many black friends back in Beaver Falls. Some classmates thought it was strange for Joe to have black friends. They began to think Joe was a little odd. This made Joe angry. He almost quit school.

Wearing the number he later made famous.

But after a while people began getting used to Joe. He began to make friends. He moved into a house with other athletes. There was music in the halls. There was plenty of good food to eat.

Joe played on the freshman team his first year at Alabama. The freshman coaches said he was doing fine. But no one paid much attention to the freshman team. All eyes were on the varsity that fall. The Crimson Tide went undefeated all year and wound up the season ranked the Number One college team in America. Over the years a lot of great football players had played

Working out in practice.

for Alabama. Joe hoped he would
be as good as the All-Americans
before him.

4
Breaking the Rules

By his second year at Alabama Joe felt more at home. Coach Bryant made him the first-string varsity quarterback. Joe immediately began helping Alabama win football games. In his first game as varsity quarterback, he threw three touchdown passes. That tied Alabama's record for touchdown passes. It was a great

35

beginning for Joe. One newspaper wrote SOPHOMORE NAMATH WOWS ALL. Joe continued to wow Alabama fans. Alabama won six games in a row. The team was still ranked Number One in the nation.

Then came the game with Georgia Tech. Coach Bryant told Joe to do a lot more passing than usual. But Joe missed his receivers many times.

Alabama lost. It was the only game that Alabama lost that season. Joe was angry that his team lost even that one game. He could hardly wait for the next season to begin.

It is very difficult for any football team to win all its games. In Joe's junior year Alabama lost two. The second loss came because Joe was not permitted to play. He had broken a training rule. Athletes must have strict training rules so they stay in shape. If they drink alcohol or stay out too late, they cannot be on the team.

Joe broke the rule against drinking. Coach Bryant found out. He called Joe over to him. He said, "Joe, I've got something to talk to you about. Let's go to my room."

They went to Bryant's room. Joe admitted he had broken the rule. The coach had to take Joe off the team for a while.

"How many days?" asked Joe.
"Not days," Bear Bryant said.

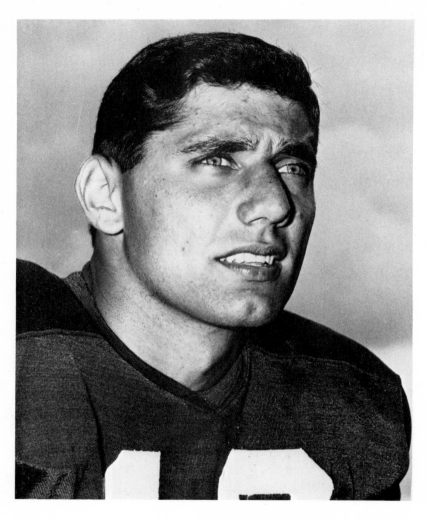

In his junior year at Alabama, Joe was suspended from the team for breaking training.

"For the year. Or forever. Or until you prove something to me."

Not playing football was the worst punishment Joe could get. He felt very bad. So did many other people. They wrote letters trying to make the coach change his mind.

Joe tried very hard to behave himself. He did so well that Bear Bryant let Joe play the next season.

5
Senior Year

It was Joe's senior year at Alabama. His punishment made him grow up. He was more serious about everything. He seemed older. He took stronger charge of the team than before.

He wanted to make up for his mistake. He felt he could do this by playing great football. And he did. With Joe leading the way, Alabama won its first three games.

Joe wore special shoes because he had to do so much running. To make his ankles stronger, he wrapped his shoes with white adhesive tape. Some people laughed at Joe's shoes.

Joe's special shoes.

So when Alabama played North Carolina State, Joe did not wear the tape on his shoes.

During the game Joe was running. He stopped suddenly. He turned and fell down. He did not get up. His face was full of pain.

Joe was helped off the field. He was taken to the dressing room. His right knee was hurt. It might not have been hurt if he had been wearing his taped shoes. The trainer put packs of ice on it to keep it from swelling. But the ice packs were not enough.

For the rest of the year, Joe was often in pain. He had what is known as water on the knee. Sometimes the doctor would put a needle into Joe's knee. He would drain off some of the liquid that was hurting Joe. This helped stop the pain.

Joe did not play very much during the next four games. Still, everyone was talking about how good Joe Namath was. It didn't matter to them that he had a hurt knee and that the doctors said he could not play.

The game with Georgia Tech was coming up. Joe and his teammates remembered their defeat two years earlier. They did not want to lose again.

Bear Bryant asked Joe if he felt he could play. His knee ached, but Joe said yes. Near the end of the

first half, the score was tied 0–0. Joe
had not yet played. Then Georgia
Tech fumbled the ball. Alabama
recovered it. Coach Bryant sent Joe
into the game.

The crowd roared with excitement.
There were less than 2 minutes left

Bear Bryant with Joe on the sidelines.

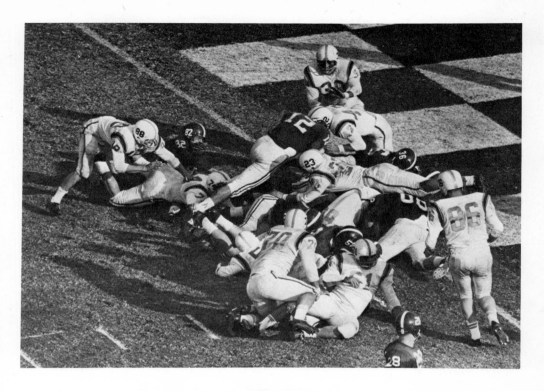

Namath (No. 12) scoring for Alabama on a quarter-back sneak from the one-yard line.

in the half. Joe completed a long
pass to Georgia Tech's one-yard line
and in 30 seconds Alabama led by
a score of 7–0. Fifty seconds later,

45

he threw for another touchdown, and the Crimson Tide led by a score of 14–0. Joe didn't play very long. But he played long enough to win the game for Alabama.

Alabama had a perfect season that year. They won every game. They were the Number One team in the nation again.

6
Orange Bowl

After the season was over, Alabama was invited to play in the Orange Bowl Game. The Orange Bowl is a big game. It is played in Florida each New Year's Day. In the afternoon before the game there is a big Orange Bowl Parade. There are many floats filled with pretty, smiling girls. Bands come from all over the state. People come a long

One of the floats in the Orange Bowl Parade.

48

way to see the parade and the game. Millions more watch it on TV.

Alabama was to play the University of Texas Longhorns, who were also undefeated. Joe had some time to rest his knee. But in practice a few days before the game, he hurt it again. A lot of people thought Joe would not be able to play.

Before the game there were fireworks. Many bands played. Trees with real oranges on them were behind one set of goalposts. Bathing beauties sat on rocks behind the other goalposts. Joe's mother came all the way from Beaver Falls to see her son play. Even President John F. Kennedy was there.

Bird's-eye view of the stadium.

Joe limped out onto the field. Jackie Gleason, the famous TV star, tossed the coin. Joe called the toss. Then he limped back to the bench.

When the game started, the Texas defense stopped Alabama cold. Soon the Texas tailback broke loose for a 79-yard touchdown, Texas kicked the extra point, and the Longhorns led by a score of 7–0. After the defense held Alabama again, Texas struck for another long touchdown. Suddenly the Crimson Tide was behind by 14 points. The Alabama fans moaned.

Then in came Joe. It became a one-man game. Joe filled the air with passes. He completed 18 of them— an Orange Bowl record—and threw for two touchdowns. He played a

Passing against Texas.

tremendous game, but it was too late. Alabama lost by a score of 21–17.

Still, after it was over, sports-writers voted for Joe as the Most Valuable Player of the Orange Bowl Game. One Texas player said, "In spite of his bad leg, Namath almost killed us. If he had been healthy, we never would have won."

Joe's days as a college quarterback were over. Now he looked forward to a career as a pro.

7
Turning Pro

The day after the Orange Bowl, Joe signed a contract to play pro football for the New York Jets. The Jets offered him more than $400,000. It would be paid over three years. Nobody could believe it. It was the most money ever paid to a professional football player.

Sonny Werblin was the owner of the Jets. He wanted a big star for the team. He thought Joe Namath would bring more fans to Shea Stadium. He knew people would be curious about a $400,000 quarterback.

New York Jets Coach Weeb Ewbank shows Joe his professional football player's contract.

Resting in the hospital after doctors operated on his knee.

The first thing the Jets did was send Joe to the hospital. He needed an operation on his right knee. It was hard for Joe to bend his knee. There was torn cartilage in his knee that was piling up and hurting him. Cartilage is soft bone. The doctors removed the damaged cartilage.

It took several months for Joe to get well. He had to do exercises to make his knee strong again. He had to lift weights with his leg. Joe worked hard at the exercises. Finally the pain went away and his knee was stronger.

Wherever Joe went, newspaper reporters asked him what he would do with all his money. He got tired of people asking him the same question over and over. Sometimes he got angry at the reporters.

Once Joe had been poor. Now he was rich. He wanted to live like a millionaire. He rented an expensive apartment in New York City. He had a white fur rug seven inches thick. He had gold faucets in his bathroom. He had a color TV.

Joe liked going out with pretty

The living room in Joe's New York apartment.

girls. He took them to fancy New York nightclubs. Some people thought he would never be a serious player. They thought that maybe he was only a playboy. They began to call him Broadway Joe.

8
Rookie Year

Joe reported to the Jets' training camp in July of 1965. He must have been a little scared. Some of his teammates were jealous that Joe was getting paid so much. He was only a rookie. How could he be that much better than they were? Joe wanted to show them he was worth the money.

The $400,000 quarterback.

Learning to be a pro quarterback is hard work. Joe had to memorize the Jets' plays from a big book. Coach Weeb Ewbank had invented the plays. There were hundreds of them.

Joe also had to learn how the opposing teams played defense. Each team plays a little differently. Joe had to watch films of games every night. It was hard to study. People followed him everywhere he went. They wanted his autograph. Joe needed more time to study.

Joe had his troubles on the field too. At first he threw his long passes too hard. They went over the heads of his receivers. He had to wear a

In the crush to get Joe's autograph, young fans tumble through a fence at the Jets' training camp.

leg brace because of his knee. It made running difficult.

But coach Ewbank didn't want Joe to do much running anyway. The Jets had plenty of good halfbacks and fullbacks who could run. Ewbank wanted Joe for the magic in his arm.

Training camp came to an end. Joe had studied hard to learn. Still, coach Ewbank thought that he was not ready to play first string with the pros. Joe did not agree.

The Jets played their opening game in Houston. A miserable Joe Namath sat on the bench. He wanted to be out on the field. The Jets lost to the Houston Oilers by a score of 27–21.

The Jets' second game was at home against the Kansas City Chiefs. Shea Stadium was packed. Most of the fans came to see Joe, but he began the game on the bench. The crowd booed.

Then the starting Jet quarterback, Mike Taliaferro, began to throw bad passes. Coach Ewbank thought he was hurt. He sent Joe into the game. The crowd cheered. And Joe did not disappoint them. He connected with his very first pass.

Though the Jets finally lost the game by a score of 14–10, everyone agreed that Joe had made a fine beginning as a pro. Coach Ewbank made him the Jets' Number One quarterback.

Hard times followed. With Joe

Namath setting up to pass in his first game as a pro.

starting, the Jets lost their next four games. It wasn't all Joe's fault. The whole team was playing badly. Reporters heard coach Ewbank screaming at his players, "You're not going to win unless you fight back. They hit you and you don't hit back. I'm getting sick and tired of it."

Ewbank was worried about his $400,000 rookie. Joe was learning fast. But maybe he wasn't yet strong enough or experienced enough. Coach Ewbank decided to put Taliaferro back in as starting quarterback.

Joe had more problems. Jets'

owner Sonny Werblin tried to get Joe to dress up more when he went places. He thought Joe should wear a jacket and a tie. Joe liked to wear sweaters and turtleneck shirts even when everyone else wore suits. Werblin thought that Joe wasn't acting grown up.

Joe wanted to show the Jets that he was more than just a kid. He did when the Jets met the Kansas City Chiefs again. Taliaferro started at quarterback. The score was close at half time. Then Ewbank sent in Joe.

As usual, the crowd cheered. For the first time Joe seemed to know just what the other team was going to do. He had also begun to learn exactly where his receivers would be. His lessons were paying off. It was Joe's best game as a pro so far. He won it for the Jets by a score of 13–0.

The next game was with the Boston Patriots. Joe played the whole game. The Jets won by a score of 30–20. Joe's old college coach, Bear Bryant, called Joe after the game. He said, "Joe, you became a pro quarterback today." The praise made Joe very happy.

For the rest of the season Joe played great football. His teammates

Handing off against the Boston Patriots.

71

came to respect him. The Jets won five of their last eight games. Joe had led a losing team to victory. He was named Rookie of the Year.

Joe's autographed picture.

9
Playing in Pain

Returning to training camp the next year was different for Joe. He was no longer a rookie trying to break in. He was the Jets' biggest star.

His main worry was his legs. Both his knees now hurt from being hit so much. What if they got hit a lot more? They might be damaged forever. That was a chance he would have to take.

The Jets played the Houston Oilers in a preseason game. A 245-

After a hard tackle it isn't easy getting up again.

pound Oiler lineman tackled Joe, smashing him to the ground. Joe lay still. Coach Ewbank ran to his side. Joe said, "My knee feels like it's just hanging there by a thread." The doctor said afterward it was only a sprain. But Joe couldn't play again for several weeks.

Joe felt he was ready by the opening game. The Jets played the Miami Dolphins. The Jets won by a score of 19–14.

The Jets played the Houston Oilers in their second game. Joe was really hot. He threw five touchdown passes. The Jets won by a score of 52–13.

The Jets rolled up one victory

Dropping back to pass against the Houston Oilers. Jets linemen block out enemy pass rushers.

after another. They won four of their first five games. They thought they might become the champions of their league that year.

Then the Jets played the Houston

Oilers for the second time. The Oilers were angry about their earlier loss. They wanted to get even. The Oilers went after Joe. They flattened him all afternoon before he could put the ball into the air. The Jets lost by a score of 24–0. Their winning streak was over. They lost six of their nine remaining games.

A lot of fans blamed Joe for the Jets' losses. They thought Joe went to too many parties and stayed up too late. They said he was too tired to play good football.

But Joe's friends knew the real reason Joe was playing poorly. He was often in pain. Joe's knees hurt him more and more. His mother wanted him to stop playing football. But Joe did not want to stop.

After the season, doctors discovered more torn cartilage in Joe's right knee. It had been there hurting him all year. It is a wonder that he had been able to play at all.

The operation Joe needed was risky. If anything went wrong, he could never play football again. He decided to take the chance. The doctors operated. They thought the operation was a success.

10
Second Place

When Joe reported for training camp at the start of his third season, his legs felt fine. But a week before the first practice game, a sharp pain went through his left knee. The doctors said not to worry, it would get better. They gave Joe medicine to stop the pain.

But Joe was upset. He wanted to get away from football for a little while. He broke training twice by leaving the camp. The first time he went to New York City for a few hours with a friend. When Joe got back to camp, he was fined $50.

A few weeks later, Joe broke training and went to New York City again. He got into an argument with a sportswriter in a nightclub. The writer said that Joe hit him. The story got into the newspapers. When Joe returned to camp, he was fined $500.

Once again, getting into trouble helped Joe grow up. He worked harder than ever at football. He played much better than he had his first two seasons.

In the past, a lot of Joe's passes had been intercepted. That was because he threw the ball even when all his receivers were covered. It is better to be tackled and lose a few yards than to throw and be intercepted. When a quarterback lets himself be tackled that way, it is called eating the ball. Joe learned to eat the ball. He threw fewer interceptions.

Best of all, the pain in Joe's knees was going away. He could run a lot better. He worked well with his two running backs, Matt Snell and Emerson Boozer. They worked out some tricky plays.

Joe had a very good season. The

Jets finished in second place in the Eastern Division of their league. But second place wasn't good enough for Joe. He wanted the Jets to be the best team in the division, the best team in the league, and the best team in the world.

Eating the ball against Oakland in the play-off.

11
AFL Champions

In the 1960's there were two professional football leagues. One was the old, established National Football League (NFL). The other was the brand-new American Football League (AFL). The Jets belonged to the new league.

At first the two leagues didn't play each other. But in 1967 they finally got together. The NFL champion Green Bay Packers met the AFL champion Kansas City Chiefs in the first Super Bowl. The Packers beat the Chiefs by a score of 35–10. The next year, in the second Super Bowl, the Packers beat the Oakland Raiders by a score of 33–14.

It was no wonder that most people thought NFL teams were much better than AFL teams. Joe Namath did not agree. He said the Jets were as good as any NFL team. He wanted a chance to prove it, and in his fourth season as a pro, he got it.

People still complained about the way Joe looked. His hair was longer than ever. He said that all the girls he knew liked men with long hair. He also grew a long, drooping mustache. Some people thought he should try to look more like a football

Talking on the field telephone.

player. They wished he would get a crew cut.

Joe did not care what people said about his looks. He figured he was paid to play football. How he looked was nobody else's business.

Some of the other Jets agreed with Joe. They grew long hair, too, and mustaches, and even beards. They said that they would not cut their hair until they had won the champion-ship.

The Jets lost only three games in the 1969 season. They won the Eastern Division title. Then they had to play the Western Division champs, the Oakland Raiders. The winner would be the AFL champions

Throwing a long pass, otherwise known as a bomb.

and get to go to the Super Bowl.

It was a close game. Oakland was winning by a score of 23–20 with eight minutes to go. Then Joe completed two passes. The Jets scored a touchdown. They won by a score of 27–23.

The Jets had won the AFL championship. They carried coach Ewbank to the showers. They threw him in with his clothes on. He was soaking wet but happy. Everybody drank champagne. Joe raised his glass high. "Super Bowl, here we come!" he said.

12
World Champions

The National Football League champions were the Baltimore Colts. They were a very powerful team. Most people expected the Colts to win the Super Bowl by a big score. It seemed certain that the Jets would be badly beaten. Everyone was sure of that except Joe Namath and the Jets.

Joe did a lot of talking before the

Calling signals in the Super Bowl.

game. He knew that Baltimore was a good team, but he believed the Jets were better. He told newspaper reporters what he thought. He told them that he knew how to beat the Colts. He said that the starting Baltimore quarterback, Earl Morrall, would only be a substitute with the Jets. Reporters asked Joe if he really thought the Jets would beat the Colts. Joe said, "I guarantee it."

The Colts got angry. Joe was only bragging, they said. One Colt even tried to beat Joe up in a restaurant. Other players had to hold the Baltimore player back.

All of a sudden, Joe stopped talking. It was time for the game.

Football fans all over the country watched Joe on television. They wondered what he would do against

Joe hands off to Matt Snell.

the mighty Colts. Could he be as good as he said he was?

At first Joe called almost nothing but running plays. That surprised the Colts. They had expected him only to pass. When Joe did throw a long pass to his deep receiver, Don Maynard, the Colts were surprised again. They were surprised all day. Time after time, Joe fooled them. He completed pass after pass. His teammates ran easily through the Baltimore defense.

At half time, the Jets led by a score of 7–0. In the second half Baltimore took too many chances trying to catch up. The Jets made some big interceptions. The whole

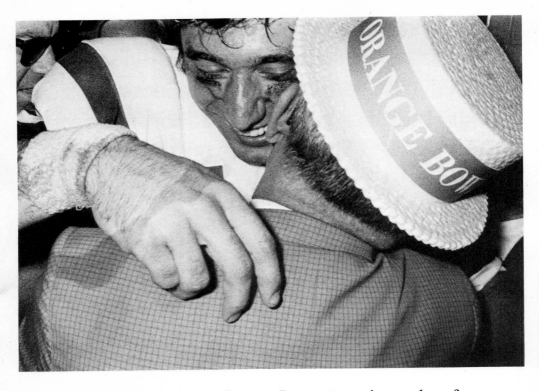

After the game a happy Joe gets a victory hug from his father.

Jets team played like champions. New York won the game by a score of 16–7.

Most fans were as surprised as the Baltimore Colts were. But Joe Namath wasn't. He had promised a victory. He was as good as his word. He had led the New York Jets to the world championship.

The Authors

Marshall and Sue Burchard are married and the parents of two children, Marshall (11) and Wendy (8). They live in New York City. Marshall, a former education editor of *Time* magazine, is presently a free-lance writer. Sue is a librarian at Trinity School.

DATE DUE	BORROWER'S NAME	ROOM NUMBER
OCT 19 92	Ed	11
FEB 2 93	Matt	9
April 30	ED	11